From Novice to Ninja Junior Kitchen Master Cookbook

Empowering Teenagers in the Kitchen with Foolproof Recipes

**Author:
Britney Kim**

INTRODUCTION

Do you want to impress your friends with home-cooked meals? You may want to whip up breakfast for your family on a Sunday morning. You may like to learn your way around the kitchen. Whatever is your reason, if you are interested in learning to cook, then this is the perfect book for you!

Teenage is exciting and this period in your life is unlike any other. It not only comes with a variety of changes but is an excellent time to pick up new skills too. You are no longer a child on one hand; on the other, you start taking your first steps to adulthood. It can sometimes be overwhelming, but you can make it easier by becoming self-reliant. Learning to cook will bring you a step closer to this goal.

You can rely on prepackaged food and takeout, but these are not only unhealthy, but the costs also quickly add up in the long run. Though they make cooking a whole lot easier, they are filled with all things unhealthy. Learning to cook is an essential life skill. When you make something by yourself from scratch, the feeling of satisfaction experienced is unlike any other. This book is designed to help you feel like a pro in the kitchen within no time. You can become the star of your own kitchen if you use the recipes given in this book properly. Cooking is not an exact science and instead, it is an art. With practice, you will become better. Also, once you know the basics of cooking, everything else is easy.

Don't worry if you have never set foot in the kitchen before. It is okay if you don't know the basics. This book will act as your guide every step of the way. It includes a compilation of simple and beginner-friendly recipes that can be whipped up in no time. What more? From now on, you will have complete control over what you are eating. The benefits of home cooking cannot be stressed enough. Also, who knows, you might discover a love for cooking by the time you are done with this book. There is no such thing as starting too early or late when it comes to learning to cook. Even if you are a beginner right now, you will get better and improve.

Safety always comes first! You must remember this at all times when you are cooking. Whether it is using the blender, microwave, oven, or even the stove, you need to know how to operate in a kitchen. If you are new to cooking, then don't hesitate to learn about all this from your parents or any other adult. You should also be careful while handling hot pans and pots and knives. Always be present and mindful of what you are doing while cooking. Maybe you can even ask an adult to supervise you the first couple of times you are working in a kitchen. Following a few safety protocols in the kitchen is needed. For instance, you must always watch what you are cooking and never leave it unattended. Always use potholders to move hot pans and pots from the stove, oven, or microwave. To prevent any hot spots while cooking, regularly stir the food. Once you are done using the knives, place them in their designated spot and don't leave them lying around. Apart from all this, make it a point to clean as you cook. This means, whenever you are done using something, clean it. Maintain a clean cooking countertop and don't leave it cluttered.

In this book, you will discover a variety of recipes divided into different categories for your convenience. From breakfast and one-pot meals to sheet pan recipes, soups, wraps, burritos, tacos, snacks, and desserts, you can whip up delicious meals like a chef. All the recipes given in this book are not only easy to cook but include simple instructions too. Don't forget to check the nutritional values of the recipes included in this book. This will make you more conscious of the food choices you make. Even if cooking seems slightly

Introduction

intimidating right now, you will not feel this way by the time you cook your way through this book. So, are you eager and excited to get started? If yes, let's begin immediately. Also, before you go, don't forget to have fun as you explore different recipes!

CHAPTER 1
SMOOTHIE RECIPES

Chocolate Banana Smoothie

Serves: 1

Nutritional values per serving: 1 smoothie

Calories: 192

Fat: 2 g

Carbohydrates: 43 g

Protein: 6 g

Ingredients:

- ½ cup milk
- ½ tablespoon honey
- 1 medium banana, cut into slices
- ½ tablespoon unsweetened cocoa powder
- 3 – 4 ice cubes

Chapter 1: Smoothie Recipes

Directions:
1. Drop the banana slices and ice cubes into the blender jar. Add honey and cocoa powder.
2. Cover the blender with its lid. Blend for 30 to 40 seconds or until the smoothie is very smooth in texture, without any banana pieces.
3. Pour into a glass and serve.

Caribbean Passion Smoothie

Serves: 1

Nutritional values per serving: 1 large smoothie

Calories: 208

Fat: 2 g

Carbohydrates: 48 g

Protein: 2 g

Ingredients:

- ½ cup mango passion fruit juice
- ¼ cup fresh or frozen peaches
- 3 – 4 ice cubes
- ½ cup fresh or frozen strawberries
- ½ cup orange sherbet

Chapter 1: Smoothie Recipes

Directions:
1. Place strawberries, ice cubes, orange sherbet, and peaches in the blender jar. Pour mango passion juice into the blender.
2. Cover the blender with its lid. Blend for about 30 to 40 seconds or until the smoothie is very smooth in texture, without having any pieces of peaches or strawberries.
3. Pour into a tall glass and serve.

Salted Caramel Milkshake

Serves: 1

Nutritional values per serving: 1 milkshake without salted caramel sauce

Calories: 571

Fat: 41 g

Carbohydrates: 43 g

Protein: 10 g

Ingredients:

- 2 scoops vanilla ice cream
- ¼ teaspoon vanilla extract
- ½ cup milk
- ½ cup lightly sweetened whipped cream 1 - 2 tablespoons salted caramel sauce plus extra to drizzle if desired

Chapter 1: Smoothie Recipes

Directions:
1. Measure 2 scoops of vanilla ice cream and place in the blender jar. Let it thaw for about 5 minutes.
2. Pour vanilla extract, salted caramel sauce, and milk into the blender.
3. Cover the blender with its lid. Blend for about 30 seconds or until smooth.
4. Pour into a glass. Place whipped cream on top. Drizzle a little salted caramel sauce on top if desired, and serve.

Mixed Berry Smoothie

Serves: 1

Nutritional values per serving:

Calories: 274

Fat: 5 g

Carbohydrates: 52 g

Protein: 11 g

Ingredients:

- ½ banana, cut into slices
- ¼ cup vanilla yogurt
- 1 ½ cups frozen mixed berries
- ⅔ cup milk

Chapter 1: Smoothie Recipes

Directions:
1. Place berries and banana slices in a blender jar.
2. Cover the blender with its lid. Blend for about 30 to 40 seconds or until the smoothie is very smooth in texture, without any banana pieces. Bits of berries taste nice.
3. Pour into a glass and serve.

Chocolate Peanut Butter Smoothie Bowl

Serves: 2

Nutritional value per serving: 1 bowl, without toppings

Calories: 459

Fat: 19 g

Carbohydrates: 62 g

Protein: 17 g

Ingredients:

- 2 peeled, frozen bananas
- 1 cup chocolate milk
- 1 cup milk
- ⅛ cup natural peanut butter
- ½ teaspoon ground cinnamon
- 1 cup original Cheerios

- ⅛ cup flaxseed meal

For toppings: Choose any
- Banana slices
- Chocolate chips
- Cheerios
- Flaxseeds
- Cacao nibs
- Shredded coconut
- Peanut butter

Directions:
1. To freeze the bananas: Peel 2 bananas. Cut the bananas into slices. Place them on a tray and freeze for about 3 hours. Freezing the bananas makes the smoothie thick.
2. Place bananas, chocolate milk, milk, peanut butter, cinnamon, cheerios, and flaxseed meal in a blender and blend until smooth.
3. Divide into 2 bowls. Place the desired toppings on top and serve right away.

CHAPTER 2
BREAKFAST RECIPES

Soft and Creamy Scrambled Eggs

Serves: 1

Nutritional value per serving:

Calories: 168

Fat: 12 g

Carbohydrates: 1 g

Protein: 13 g

Ingredients:
- 2 large eggs
- 1 teaspoon butter
- Salt to taste
- Pepper to taste

Chapter 2: Breakfast Recipes

Directions:
1. Crack eggs into a bowl. Add pepper and salt and whisk lightly with a fork until well combined.
2. Place the non-stick pan over low heat. You must keep the heat down.
3. Add butter. When the butter melts, add the egg mixture. Do not stir for 20 seconds.
4. Using a silicone spatula or a wooden spoon, stir lightly. Lift and fold the egg over itself from the bottom of the pan.
5. Do not stir for another 5 – 8 seconds. Lift and fold the egg over itself from the bottom of the pan.
6. Repeat the previous step a couple of times until the eggs are cooked soft overall and runny at different spots. Turn off the heat.
7. Stir lightly and serve immediately.
8. If, at any time, the eggs are cooking too quickly, take the pan off the heat for a few seconds.

Savory Cheese Muffins

Serves: 22

Nutritional values per serving: 1 muffin

Calories: 275

Fat: 18 g

Carbohydrates: 20 g

Protein: 8.1 g

Ingredients:

- 6 tablespoons salted butter
- 4 cups grated cheddar cheese
- 4 cloves garlic, peeled, minced, crushed
- 4 cups all-purpose flour
- 1 teaspoon baking soda
- 3 teaspoons baking powder

Chapter 2: Breakfast Recipes

- 1 teaspoon salt
- 2 cups milk
- 3 tablespoons vegetable oil
- 2 cloves garlic, peeled, crushed
- 2 large eggs, lightly beaten
- ½ cup sour cream or plain yogurt
- ½ cup minced chopped fresh parsley

Directions:

1. Take your parent's help and set the oven temperature to 350°F. Preheat the oven.
2. Also, learn from your parents how to use a microwave. Combine minced garlic and butter in a microwave-safe container and melt it in a microwave for about 30 seconds.
3. Brush this mixture into the muffin cups of 2 muffin pans of 12 counts each. Make sure each hole has a bit of garlic in it. Do not use all of it; keep some to use later.
4. Combine flour, baking soda, baking powder, and salt in a bowl.
5. Combine milk, oil, crushed garlic, eggs, yogurt, and parsley in another bowl.
6. Add the milk mixture into the bowl of the flour mixture and stir until well combined.
7. Add cheese and fold until just combined. Folding means stirring lightly. Spoon the batter into the muffin cups. Fill up to ¾ the muffin cups.
8. Place the muffin pans in the oven and set the timer for about 25 minutes or until golden brown and firm on top.
9. Take out the muffins from the pans and place them on a cooling rack. Brush the butter garlic mixture on top, which was set aside.

10. In the refrigerator, place extra muffins in an airtight container at room temperature for about 3 days or about a week. Make sure to warm them up in a microwave before serving.

Chapter 2: Breakfast Recipes

Berry Chia Pudding

Serves: 1

Nutritional values per serving: 1 glass

Calories: 343

Fat: 15 g

Carbohydrates: 39 g

Protein: 14 g

Ingredients:

- ¼ cup blackberries
- ¼ cup raspberries
- ⅓ cup diced mango
- 2 tablespoons chia seeds
- ½ teaspoon vanilla extract
- ⅛ cup granola

- ½ cup unsweetened milk of your preference
- ½ tablespoon pure maple syrup
- ¼ cup whole-milk plain Greek yogurt

Directions:

1. Place half of each – the mango, blackberries, and raspberries in a blender jar. Pour in the milk. Cover the jar and blend until smooth.
2. Pour the blended berries into a bowl. Add chia seeds, vanilla, and maple syrup and stir until well combined.
3. Cover the bowl and chill all night. You can make it ahead of time and use it within 3 days.
4. Place half of the chia pudding in a glass. Scatter a little of the remaining blackberries, raspberries, and mango over the pudding.
5. Now place the yogurt over the fruits. Place the remaining pudding over the yogurt.
6. Scatter the remaining fruits over the yogurt layer. Sprinkle granola on top and serve immediately.

Chapter 2: Breakfast Recipes

Yogurt Parfait

Serves: 2

Nutritional values per serving: 1 parfait

Calories: 291

Fat: 6 g

Carbohydrates: 46 g

Protein: 15 g

Ingredients:

- 1 cup plain yogurt
- ½ cup strawberries
- ¼ cup raspberries
- ¼ cup blueberries
- ½ ripe mango, peeled, cubed
- 1 tablespoon maple syrup

- ½ cup granola

Directions:

1. Combine maple syrup and yogurt.
2. Take 2 parfait glasses or bowls. Make layers of yogurt, granola, berries, and mango in a colorful manner.
3. You can have alternate layers of yogurt. You can mix up the fruits and place them between the yogurt layers along with granola or place one particular fruit between the yogurt layers.
4. Enjoy right away, or else the granola will get soggy.

Chapter 2: Breakfast Recipes

Pancakes

Serves: 4

Nutritional values per serving: 1 pancake, without toppings

Calories: 127

Fat: 2 g

Carbohydrates: 22 g

Protein: 5 g

Ingredients:

- ¾ cup flour
- ½ tablespoon sugar
- 1 teaspoon unsalted butter, melted
- 10 tablespoons milk
- ½ tablespoon baking powder
- ¼ teaspoon salt

- ¼ teaspoon vanilla extract
- 1 small egg

Directions:

1. Add flour, sugar, baking powder, and salt into a mixing bowl and stir until well combined.
2. Make a well in the center of the flour mixture.
3. Place vanilla, melted butter, and milk in the well. Crack the egg into the well.
4. Stir until the batter is smooth and well combined. If you are familiar with using an electric hand mixer, you can mix the batter using it. Ensure you have an adult or parent around you when using the electric hand mixer.
5. Place a skillet or pan over medium-high heat. Spray the pan with some cooking oil spray. You can use butter if desired.
6. Pour ¼ of the batter (about a spoonful) onto the griddle. If your skillet is large enough, you can make 2 pancakes at a time.
7. Soon bubbles will be visible on top of the pancake. You will notice the edges are slightly brown. Lift a bit of the pancake with a spatula and check if it is browned as you prefer.
8. If it is browned, slide the spatula completely underneath the pancake and flip sides. Cook the other side for 1 – 2 minutes, or cook as you prefer.
9. Remove the pancake onto a plate. Serve with toppings of your choice.
10. Cook the remaining pancakes until all the batter is gone.

Banana, Oat, and Blueberry Waffle

Serves: 4

Nutritional values per serving: 1 waffle, without toppings

Calories: 161

Fat: 3 g

Carbohydrates: 29 g

Protein: 6 g

Ingredients:

- ½ cup rolled oats
- 1 teaspoon baking powder
- ½ cup whole-wheat flour
- ½ teaspoon ground cinnamon
- 1 ripe banana
- ½ cup blueberries

- ½ cup milk
- 1 egg

Directions:

1. Place oats in a blender. Process until finely powdered.
2. Add cinnamon, flour, and baking powder and process until well combined.
3. Add banana, egg, and milk and process until smooth.
4. Pour the batter into a bowl. Add blueberries and stir.
5. Set up the waffle iron with an adult's supervision and preheat it according to the manufacturer's instructions.
6. Spray some cooking spray in the waffle maker. Pour ¼ of the batter into the waffle maker. Cook for 3 – 4 minutes or until crisp.
7. Remove the waffle and serve with toppings of your choice.
8. Similarly, make the remaining waffles.

CHAPTER 3
SOUP RECIPES

Beef Soup

Serves: 3

Nutritional value per serving: 1 ¼ cups

Calories: 142

Fat: 5 g

Carbohydrates: 16 g

Protein: 10 g

Ingredients:

- ¼ pound ground beef
- ½ can (from a 14.5 ounce can) of stewed tomatoes
- ½ cup canned tomato sauce
- ¼ teaspoon sugar
- 1 cup water

Chapter 3: Soup Recipes

- ½ package (from a 10 ounces package) of frozen mixed vegetables
- ½ envelope of onion soup mix

Directions:

1. Place a soup pot over medium heat. Add beef and stir. As you stir, break the meat into smaller pieces. As the beef cooks, it will change its color. Also, fat will be released.
2. When the beef is not pink anymore, drain off the fat from the pot.
3. Stir in stewed tomatoes, tomato sauce, sugar, water, mixed vegetables, and onion soup mix.
4. Turn the heat low when the soup starts boiling, and cover the pot. Cook until vegetables are tender. Stir occasionally.
5. Ladle into soup bowls and serve.

Chicken Noodle Soup

Serves: 4

Nutritional values per serving: 1 cup

Calories: 188

Fat: 2 g

Carbohydrates: 27 g

Protein: 15 g

Ingredients:

- 4 cups water mixed with 2 chicken bouillon cubes or chicken broth or chicken bone broth
- 1 large chicken breast half, cut into small pieces
- ½ bag (from a 12 ounces bag) of frozen vegetable medley
- ½ tablespoon fresh lemon juice (optional)
- 4 ounces uncooked whole-wheat rotini noodles

Chapter 3: Soup Recipes

- Salt to taste
- 1 tablespoon chopped parsley (optional)
- Pepper to taste

Directions:

1. Add broth or water with chicken bouillon cubes into a soup pot. Add the chicken as well.
2. Now place the pot over high heat. When the chicken gets cooked (it will not look pink), add in the noodles. After about 3 minutes, stir in the frozen vegetables. Add salt and pepper to taste.
3. When the pasta is cooked, turn off the heat. Add lemon juice and parsley and stir.
4. Ladle into soup bowls and serve.

Spaghetti and Meatball Soup

Serves: 3

Nutritional values per serving: 1 bowl

Calories: 100

Fat: 3 g

Carbohydrates: 16 g

Protein: 30 g

Ingredients:
- ½ tablespoon olive oil
- ½ cup chopped onion
- Salt to salt
- 1 can (14.5 ounces) beef broth
- 2 ounces uncooked spaghetti, break into smaller pieces

- ½ package (from a 16 ounces package) of frozen cocktail size Italian style beef meatballs
- ¼ teaspoon dried basil
- Pepper to taste
- 1 can (14.5 ounces) diced tomatoes with basil, oregano, and garlic

Directions:

1. Add olive oil to a soup pot. Place the soup pot over medium heat. Add onion, meatballs, pepper, salt, and basil when the oil is hot. Stir occasionally until the meatballs turn light brown.
2. Stir in the broth. Do not drain the juices from the can of tomatoes. Add the tomatoes to the pot and stir. When it starts boiling, add spaghetti and cook for about 9 to 10 minutes or until it is cooked.
3. Divide the soup into three bowls and serve. Make sure there's an equal number of meatballs in each bowl.

Pizza Soup

Serves: 2

Nutritional values per serving: 1 bowl, without serving options

Calories: 232

Fat: 11.6 g

Carbohydrates: 25.1 g

Protein: 8.1 g

Ingredients:

- ½ red onion, diced
- ½ red bell pepper, diced
- ½ green bell pepper, diced
- 2 cloves garlic, peeled, minced
- 1 medium Portobello mushroom, cut into ½ inch pieces
- ¼ teaspoon salt or to taste

- ½ teaspoon fennel seeds
- 1 can (14 ounces) of fire-roasted crushed tomatoes with their liquid
- ¼ cup parmesan cheese plus extra to serve
- 1 tablespoon olive oil
- ½ tablespoon dried oregano
- ½ jar (from a 15 ounces jar) of pizza sauce
- 2 cups vegetable broth
- Chopped fresh basil leaves to garnish (optional)

To serve: Optional

- Crusty bread
- Garlic bread
- Croutons

Directions:

1. Place a soup pot over medium-high heat. Add oil to the pot. Add onion and stir-fry for about a minute when the oil gets hot.
2. Stir in the bell pepper and mushrooms and cook for a few minutes.
3. Stir in the garlic, salt, fennel, oregano, and red pepper flakes. Cook for another minute.
4. Stir in the pizza sauce, vegetable broth, and tomatoes. When it starts boiling, turn down the heat and let it boil gently for about 8 to 10 minutes. Stir occasionally.
5. Add cheese and give it a good stir. Once the cheese melts, turn off the heat.
6. Divide the soup into two bowls. Garnish with parmesan and basil leaves.
7. You can serve it as it is or with any suggested options.

Turkey Chili Taco Soup

Serves: 4 – 5

Nutritional values per serving: 1 ¼ cups, without toppings

Calories: 225

Fat: 2 g

Carbohydrates: 31.5 g

Protein: 22 g

Ingredients:
- ½ bell pepper, diced
- 10.4 ounces 99% lean ground turkey
- ¾ cup drained, canned, or frozen corn kernels
- ½ cup tomato sauce
- 3 – 4 teaspoons taco seasoning or as per your taste
- Cooking oil spray

Chapter 3: Soup Recipes

- ½ medium onion, chopped
- ½ can (from 10-ounce can) Rotel tomatoes with green chilies
- ¾ cup drained, cooked, or canned kidney beans
- ½ can (from 16 ounces can) of fat-free refried beans
- 1 ¼ cups chicken broth

Directions:

1. Place a soup pot over medium heat. Spray some cooking oil spray into the pot.
2. Add turkey into the pot and stir occasionally. As the turkey cooks, it will change color.
3. When it doesn't look pink anymore, stir in the bell pepper and onion. Cook for a couple of minutes.
4. Stir in corn, tomatoes, tomato sauce, refried beans, chicken broth, and taco seasoning.
5. When it starts boiling, cover the pot with a lid. Turn down the heat to low and cook for about 12 – 15 minutes, stirring occasionally.
6. Turn off the heat. Serve in bowls with your favorite toppings.

CHAPTER 4
SALAD RECIPES

Italian Bread Salad with Olives

Serves: 4-5

Preparation time: 10 minutes

Cooking time: 12 – 15 minutes

Total time: 25 minutes

Nutritional value per serving: 1 cup

Calories: 316

Fat: 21 g

Carbohydrates: 31 g

Protein: 5 g

Ingredients:

- 5 cups cubed ciabatta bread (½ inch cubes)
- 2 cloves garlic, peeled, minced
- 2 tablespoons balsamic vinegar

Chapter 4: Salad Recipes

- 1 large tomato, chopped
- A handful of fresh basil, chopped
- ⅛ cup shredded parmesan cheese
- 6 tablespoons olive oil
- ⅛ teaspoon pepper or to taste
- ⅛ teaspoon salt or to taste
- ⅛ cup sliced olives
- 1 tablespoon chopped fresh Italian parsley

Directions:

1. Preheat the oven to 350° F.
2. Add bread cubes into a bowl.
3. Combine garlic, oil, and pepper in another bowl. Take 1 ½ tablespoons of the oil mixture and pour over the bread cubes. Toss well.
4. Add tomato, vinegar, salt, olives, parsley, and basil to the remaining oil, and mix well.
5. Place the bread cubes in a baking dish and spread them evenly. Place the baking dish in the oven and set the timer for about 12 to 15 minutes or until crispy and slightly brown.
6. Take out the baking dish and cool for about 6 – 8 minutes.
7. Add the tomato mixture and toss well. Garnish with cheese and serve.

Chicken Caesar Salad

Serves: 3

Nutritional values per serving: 2 cups

Calories: 306

Fat: 16 g

Carbohydrates: 10.3 g

Protein: 29.4 g

Ingredients:

For the salad:

- 1 ½ cups roasted, skinless, shredded chicken
- ½ cup red bell pepper strips
- 10 ounces torn lettuce leaves (about 5 ½ - 6 cups)
- ¼ cup grated fresh parmesan cheese
- ¾ cup plain croutons

Chapter 4: Salad Recipes

For the dressing:
- 2 teaspoons fresh lemon juice
- 1 teaspoon Dijon mustard
- Salt to taste
- ½ clove garlic, minced
- 1 ½ tablespoons olive oil
- 1 teaspoon Worcestershire sauce
- A pinch of sugar
- A pinch of pepper

Directions:
1. To make the dressing: Add lemon juice, mustard, salt, garlic, oil, Worcestershire sauce, sugar, and pepper into a small jar. Fasten the lid of the jar and shake vigorously for a few seconds until well combined.
2. Add chicken, lettuce, and bell pepper into a bowl and whisk well.
3. Add the dressing and mix well.
4. Add cheese and croutons. Stir and serve right away.

Waldorf Salad

Serves: 2

Nutritional values per serving: ½ recipe

Calories: 301

Fat: 22 g

Carbohydrates: 25 g

Protein: 6 g

Ingredients:

For the dressing:

- 3 tablespoons mayonnaise
- ¼ teaspoon salt
- ½ tablespoon lemon juice
- Freshly ground black pepper to taste

For the salad:

- ½ cup seedless red grapes, halved, or ⅛ cup raisins
- ½ cup chopped walnuts
- 1 sweet apple, cored, chopped
- ½ cup thinly sliced celery
- 4 cups shredded lettuce leaves

Directions:

1. To make the dressing: Add mayonnaise, salt, lemon juice, and pepper into a medium size bowl and stir until well combined.
2. Add fruits, walnuts, and celery and stir until well combined.
3. Place 2 cups of lettuce leaves on each serving plate.
4. Divide the salad equally and place it over the lettuce.
5. Serve.

Berry Fruit Salad

Serves: 3

Nutritional values per serving: 1 ⅓ cups

Calories: 45

Fat: 0 g

Carbohydrates: 11 g

Protein: 1 g

Ingredients:

- ½ teaspoon white sugar
- ½ cup quartered strawberries
- ½ cup fresh blackberries
- ½ cup fresh blueberries
- ½ cup fresh raspberries

Chapter 4: Salad Recipes

Directions:
1. Place all the berries and sugar in a bowl and toss well.
2. Serve.

Classic Pea Salad

Serves: 4

Nutritional values per serving: ⅓ cup

Calories: 265

Fat: 21 g

Carbohydrates: 11 g

Protein: 9 g

Ingredients:

- ¼ cup sour cream
- ½ tablespoon granulated sugar
- ⅛ teaspoon salt or to taste
- 2 cups frozen peas, thawed
- ⅓ heaping cup of cubed, sharp cheddar cheese
- 2 tablespoons mayonnaise

Chapter 4: Salad Recipes

- 1 teaspoon apple cider vinegar
- A pinch of pepper
- 1 small red onion, diced
- 4 slices pre-cooked crispy bacon, crumbled

Directions:

1. Add sour cream, sugar, salt, mayonnaise, apple cider vinegar, and pepper into a bowl and stir until well combined.
2. Stir in peas, cheese, onion, and most of the bacon. Chill for an hour.
3. Serve garnished with remaining bacon.

CHAPTER 5
WRAP, BURRITO, TACO AND QUESADILLA RECIPES

Chicken Napa Wraps

Serves: 3

Nutritional values per serving: 1 wrap

Calories: 396

Fat: 22 g

Carbohydrates: 30 g

Protein: 18 g

Ingredients:

- 2 ounces of cream cheese
- 3 tablespoons shredded cheddar cheese
- 1 ½ teaspoons mustard
- 4 ounces of cooked chicken, diced
- 2 ounces sour cream
- ½ tablespoon thinly sliced green onion

- 3 flour tortillas (8 inches each)
- ¾ cup shredded Napa cabbage

Directions:
1. Add cream cheese, cheddar cheese, mustard, sour cream, and green onion into a bowl and stir until well combined.
2. Mix 2 tablespoons of the cream cheese mixture on a tortilla. Repeat this step with the remaining tortillas and cream cheese mixture.
3. Divide the chicken into 3 equal portions. Spread one portion of chicken on each tortilla. Scatter ¼ cup of Napa cabbage on each tortilla.
4. Roll each tortilla tightly and serve.

Crunchy Tuna Wraps

Serves: 4

Nutritional values per serving: 1 wrap

Calories: 312

Fat: 10 g

Carbohydrates: 34 g

Protein: 23 g

Ingredients:

- 2 pouches (6.4 ounces each) of light tuna in water
- ½ cup sliced green onions
- ½ red bell pepper, diced
- ½ cup finely chopped celery
- ½ cup chopped water chestnuts
- 4 tablespoons low-fat mayonnaise

- 4 spinach tortillas (8 inches each) at room temperature
- 4 teaspoons prepared mustard
- 2 cups shredded lettuce

Directions:

1. Drain the tuna and add it to a bowl. Add green onion, bell pepper, celery, water chestnuts, mayonnaise, and mustard into a bowl and stir.
2. Place the tortillas on a large serving platter. Distribute equally the tuna filling into four parts and spread one part on each tortilla.
3. Roll each tortilla tightly and serve.

Chipotle Bean Burritos

Serves: 3

Nutritional values per serving:

Calories: 361

Fat: 10.3 g

Carbohydrates: 52.2 g

Protein: 16.8 g

Ingredients:

- 1 ½ teaspoons canola oil
- ¼ teaspoon chipotle chili powder
- 3 tablespoons water
- ½ can (from 15 ounces can) of kidney beans, drained
- ½ can (a 15-ounce can) of black beans, drained
- 2 low-fat flour tortillas (10 inches each)

Chapter 5: Wrap, Burrito, Taco And Quesadilla Recipes

- ¾ cup chopped plum tomatoes
- 3 tablespoons chopped green onion
- ½ cup thinly sliced lettuce
- 1 ½ tablespoons chilled fresh salsa
- ⅛ teaspoon salt
- 2 small cloves garlic, minced
- ½ cup reduced fat shredded 4 - cheese Mexican blend
- 3 tablespoons light sour cream

Directions:

1. Take a non-stick pan and place it over medium heat. Add oil to the pan. Add garlic and stir for about 20 – 25 seconds when the oil is hot.
2. Add chili powder and salt and stir constantly for a few seconds. Add water and beans and stir.
3. Turn the heat low when it boils, and cover the pan with a lid. Simmer for about 10 minutes. Turn off the heat and add salsa. Mix well and slightly mash the beans with a fork.
4. You will find instructions for heating the tortillas on the package. Well, follow those instructions and warm the tortillas.
5. Divide the bean mixture into 3 equal portions and place one portion on the center of each tortilla. Slightly spread the mixture in the center.
6. Divide the cheese, tomatoes, lettuce, green onion, and sour cream and place over the bean mixture.
7. How to fold a burrito: Fold the left and right sides of the tortillas inwards over a part of the filling. Now lift the side that is nearest to you, and place it over the filling. Start rolling it along with the filling until you reach the other end. Place it with the seam side facing down.
8. Serve.

Beef Burrito

Serves: 3

Nutritional values per serving: 1 burrito, without toppings

Calories: 659

Fat: 26 g

Carbohydrates: 74 g

Protein: 31 g

Ingredients:

- ½ pound lean ground beef
- ¾ cup refried beans
- 1 ½ cups cooked rice
- ¾ cup shredded cheddar cheese
- ½ packet taco seasoning mix
- 6 tablespoons corn kernels

Chapter 5: Wrap, Burrito, Taco And Quesadilla Recipes

- 3 large flour tortillas (10 inches each)

Optional toppings:
- Shredded lettuce
- Finely chopped red onion
- Sour cream
- Salsa
- Chopped cilantro
- Chopped avocado or guacamole
- Chopped tomatoes

Directions:
1. With your parent's help, set the oven temperature to 350°F. Preheat the oven.
2. Place beef in a non-stick pan. Sprinkle taco seasoning over the beef. Place the pan over medium heat.
3. Stir often. As you stir, break the meat into smaller pieces. Soon the beef will change its color from pink to brown.
4. Turn off the heat.
5. You can mash black beans and use them if you do not have refried beans.
6. Place ¼ cup of beans on the center of each tortilla, along the diameter. Place ½ cup of rice, ⅓ of the beef, 2 tablespoons of corn, and ¼ cup of cheese over the beans on each tortilla.
7. Folding the burrito is explained in the previous recipe.
8. Grease a baking dish with some cooking oil spray. Place the burritos in the baking dish with the seam side down.
9. Keep the dish covered with foil and place it in the oven. Set the timer for 25 minutes.
10. Serve.

Tofu Tacos

Serves: 2

Nutritional values per serving: 2 tacos without Pico de Gallo or guacamole

Calories: 394

Fat: 18 g

Carbohydrates: 42 g

Protein: 19 g

Ingredients:
- 1 tablespoon taco seasoning or to taste
- 8 ounces extra-firm tofu
- ¼ cup chopped onion
- ¾ cup drained, canned, or cooked black beans, rinsed
- ¼ cup chopped cilantro

Chapter 5: Wrap, Burrito, Taco And Quesadilla Recipes

- A handful of shredded cabbage
- 1 ½ tablespoons extra-virgin olive oil, divided
- 1 large clove garlic, peeled, minced
- 1 teaspoon cider vinegar
- 4 corn tortillas warmed
- Pico de Gallo or guacamole optional

Directions:

1. Take some paper towels and pat the tofu until nice and dry. Chop the tofu into ½ inch cubes.
2. Place tofu in a bowl. Sprinkle taco seasoning over the tofu and toss well.
3. Take a non-stick pan and place it over medium heat. Add 1 tablespoon of oil to the pan.
4. Wait for the oil to heat up. Add onion to the pan and stir on and off for a few minutes.
5. Stir in the garlic. Keep on stirring for about 40 – 50 seconds. Turn up the heat to medium-high. Add tofu and mix well. Do not stir for about 2 minutes until the underside turns light brown. Now stir and repeat this with the remaining sides. The tofu needs to be brown all over.
6. Once the tofu turns brown, add in the beans. Give it a good stir. Once the beans are heated well, turn off the heat.
7. Add vinegar and cilantro and stir.
8. Make four equal portions of the tofu mixture and place one portion on each tortilla.
9. Scatter a little cabbage on each tortilla. Spoon some Pico de Gallo on each and serve.

Black Bean Tacos

Serves: 3

Nutritional values per serving: 1 taco

Calories: 162

Fat: 4.5 g

Carbohydrates: 25.9 g

Protein: 6.3 g

Ingredients:

- ¾ cup canned or cooked black beans, rinsed, drained
- 2 – 3 tablespoons of liquid from the canned or cooked black beans
- ¼ teaspoon garlic powder
- 3 hard corn tacos shells
- ⅛ teaspoon salt or to taste

For the toppings:
- ½ avocado, peeled, pitted, thinly sliced
- 3 tablespoons salsa
- Hot sauce to taste (optional)
- ½ small red onion, thinly sliced
- 1 tablespoon chopped fresh cilantro leaves

Directions:
1. With your parent's help, set the oven temperature to 350°F. Preheat the oven.
2. Place black beans, salt, garlic powder, and canned or cooked liquid from the black beans in a pan.
3. Place the pan over low heat. Stir often and let it simmer for about 7 – 8 minutes or until all the liquid has been absorbed.
4. While the beans are cooking, place the taco shells on a baking sheet. Place it in the oven and bake (time according to the instructions given on the package). It may be 3 to 4 minutes.
5. Distribute the black beans equally and place them inside the taco shells. Place a tablespoon of salsa in each shell. Divide the avocado, cilantro, and onions equally and place them in the taco shells.
6. Serve right away.

Quesadillas

Serves: 2

Nutritional values per serving: 1 quesadilla, without toppings

Calories: 460

Fat: 27.5 g

Carbohydrates: 31.3 g

Protein: 7.9 g

Ingredients:
- 2 whole-wheat tortillas (8 inches each)
- ½ cup cooked or canned black beans or pinto beans, rinsed, drained
- 2 tablespoons chopped red onion or green onion
- 2 teaspoons avocado oil or butter or extra-virgin olive oil
- 1 cup freshly grated cheddar cheese

- 2 tablespoons chopped red bell pepper or roasted red bell pepper from the jar or
- 6 thinly sliced cherry tomatoes
- 2 tablespoons chopped pickled jalapeño (optional)

To serve: Use any

- Salsa
- Guacamole
- Pico de Gallo
- Thinly sliced avocado
- Hot sauce
- Sour cream
- Chopped fresh cilantro

Directions:

1. Plac|e a skillet over medium heat.
2. Place a tortilla in the skillet. Let the tortilla heat for 12 – 15 seconds. Flip the tortilla over and let the other side heat for about 12 – 15 seconds.
3. Sprinkle ¼ cup of cheese on one half of the tortilla. Scatter half the beans, onion, bell pepper, and jalapeño over the cheese.
4. Lift the other half of the tortilla, fold it in the middle, and place it over the filling. So now you have a semi-circle shape (half-moon). Press the tortilla lightly.
5. Brush ½ teaspoon of oil on top of the tortilla and flip sides. Brush ½ teaspoon of oil on top of the tortilla.
6. When the underside is nice and crisp, flip the quesadilla over. Cook the other side until crisp. Remove the quesadilla onto a plate. Cut into wedges and serve.
7. Similarly, make the other quesadilla (follow steps 2-6).

Chicken Quesadilla

Serves: 3

Nutritional values per serving: 1 quesadilla

Calories: 478

Fat: 41 g

Carbohydrates: 16 g

Protein: 12 g

Ingredients:

- ½ cup mayonnaise
- ⅛ teaspoon garlic salt
- 3 flour tortillas (8 inches each)
- 1 cup shredded chicken, seasoned
- ¼ teaspoon taco seasoning or to taste
- 1 teaspoon hot sauce

- 1 cup shredded Mexican cheese
- 3 teaspoons olive oil or any cooking oil

Directions:
1. Add mayonnaise, garlic salt, taco seasoning, and hot sauce into a bowl and stir until well combined.
2. Place a non-stick pan over medium heat.
3. Spread some mayonnaise mixture on a tortilla. Place the tortilla in the pan. Place ⅓ cup of chicken on half the tortilla, spreading it evenly. Sprinkle ⅓ cup of cheese over the chicken.
4. Lift the other half of the tortilla, fold it in the middle, and place it over the filling. So now you have a semi-circle shape (half-moon). Press the tortilla lightly.
5. Brush ½ teaspoon of oil on top of the tortilla and flip sides. Brush ½ teaspoon of oil on top of the tortilla.
6. When the underside is nice and crisp, flip the quesadilla over. Cook the other side until crisp. Remove the quesadilla onto a plate. Cut into wedges and serve.
7. Similarly, make the other 2 quesadillas (follow steps 3 – 6).

CHAPTER 6
PIZZA, SANDWICHES, AND BURGERS

The Perfect Basic Burger

Serves: 8

Nutritional value per serving: 1 burger without toppings

Calories: 317

Fat: 18 g

Carbohydrates: 10 g

Protein: 27 g

Ingredients:
- 2 large eggs
- 1 teaspoon ground black pepper
- 1 cup fine dry breadcrumbs
- 1 teaspoon salt
- 2 pounds of ground beef

Serving options:

Chapter 6: Pizza, Sandwiches, And Burgers

- Hamburger buns
- Lettuce or spinach
- Cheese slices
- Tomato slices
- Mayonnaise
- Any other condiment of your choice

Directions:
1. Combine eggs, pepper, and salt in a bowl using a fork.
2. Mix in breadcrumbs and beef using your hands until well combined. Make sure not to over-mix.
3. Divide the meat mixture into 8 equal portions and shape each into a burger.
4. To serve: Cook the burgers on both sides either in a pan or bake in an oven.
5. To cook in an oven: Set the oven to broil mode seeking an adult's help, and preheat the oven. Place the burgers on a baking sheet and place the baking sheet in the oven. Broil for 6 – 8 minutes. Turn the burgers over and cook the other side for 6 – 8 minutes or until the internal temperature of the burgers shows around 160 - 165° F. To check the temperature, insert an instant-read or meat thermometer inside a burger.
6. To cook in a pan: Place a large pan over medium heat. When the pan is hot, place the burgers in the pan and cook for 6 – 8 minutes on each side or until the internal temperature of the burgers shows around 160 - 165° F on the meat thermometer.
7. Extra burgers can be frozen. Cool the burgers. Wrap each burger individually in foil and put them in a freezer bag. Freeze until ready to use. You can also store the cooled burgers in an airtight container in the refrigerator for 3 – 4 days.

8. Serve with any of the suggested serving options or toppings of your choice.

Chapter 6: Pizza, Sandwiches, And Burgers

Spicy Black Bean Burgers with Chipotle Mayo

Serves: 2

Nutritional values per serving: 1 burger with bun and a tablespoon of chipotle mayonnaise

Calories: 343

Fat: 13 g

Carbohydrates: 41 g

Protein: 11 g

Ingredients:

For spicy chipotle mayonnaise:
- ½ tablespoon chopped chipotle chili in adobo sauce
- 5 teaspoons mayonnaise

For the burgers:

- ¼ red bell pepper, roughly chopped
- A handful of fresh cilantro leaves chopped
- ¼ cup quick-cooking oats
- ½ teaspoon hot sauce
- A pinch of salt or as per your taste
- 2 whole-wheat potato rolls
- ¾ cup cooked or canned black beans, rinsed, drained
- ¼ cup roughly chopped scallions
- 2 cloves garlic, peeled, grated
- 1 small egg
- ½ tablespoon ground cumin
- ½ medium Hass avocado, thinly sliced

Directions:

1. To make spicy chipotle mayonnaise, Add chili and mayonnaise into a small bowl and stir.
2. To make black bean burgers: Spread the beans over 2 – 3 layers of paper towels. Take 2 layers of paper towels and pat the beans dry.
3. Place the beans in a bowl and mash the beans using a fork or a potato masher.
4. Place scallions, bell pepper, garlic, and cilantro in the food processor bowl or blender. Give short pulses until finely chopped. Take an adult's help to do this step.
5. Crack the egg into the food processor bowl. Also, add the hot sauce, oats, salt, and cumin and give short pulses until well incorporated.
6. Transfer the mixture to the bowl with mashed beans. Mix with your hand until well combined. If the mixture is too wet, add a teaspoon of oats.
7. Make 2 equal parts of the mixture. Shape each part into a patty. You can dip your hands in water while you shape the patty. It will not get stuck to your hands.

Chapter 6: Pizza, Sandwiches, And Burgers

8. Place a sheet of parchment paper on a plate. Place the burgers on the baking sheet in the freezer for 2 hours.
9. Place a non-stick pan over medium heat. Spray some cooking oil spray into the pan. Place the burgers in the pan. Cook until the underside is golden brown (about 6 to 7 minutes). Turn the burgers over and cook the other side until golden brown (about 6 to 7 minutes).
10. Split the rolls and place a burger on the bottom half of each roll. Spoon chipotle mayonnaise over the burger. Place avocado slices. Cover with the top half of the rolls and serve.

Mini Bagel Pizzas

Serves: 2

Nutritional values per serving: 2 mini pizzas

Calories: 232

Fat: 6 g

Carbohydrates: 30 g

Protein: 14 g

Ingredients:

- 4 mini bagels, split
- 3 tablespoons shredded pizza cheese blend
- 2 tablespoons pizza sauce
- 8 slices turkey pepperoni

Chapter 6: Pizza, Sandwiches, And Burgers

Directions:

1. With your parent's help, set the oven temperature to 425°F. Preheat the oven. Place a sheet of aluminum foil or parchment paper on a baking sheet.
2. Place the bagels on the baking sheet with the cut side facing on top.
3. Spread a little pizza sauce in a thin layer on the cut part of each bagel half.
4. Scatter cheese on top. Lay 2 pepperoni slices on each bagel in half. Place the baking sheet in the oven and set the timer for about 6 minutes or until the cheese melts and is brown at a few spots.
5. Serve.

Rainbow Pizzas

Serves: 2

Nutritional values per serving: 1 pizza

Calories: 283

Fat: 6 g

Carbohydrates: 40 g

Protein: 8 g

Ingredients:

- 2 whole-wheat pita bread
- ⅓ cup grated pizza cheese
- 3 tablespoons pizza sauce
- ¼ cup coarsely grated gold sweet potato (orange-colored)
- A handful of broccoli florets, finely chopped
- ¼ cup finely chopped, canned baby beetroots

Chapter 6: Pizza, Sandwiches, And Burgers

- 1.75 ounces grape tomatoes, thinly sliced
- ¼ cup frozen corn kernels
- ¼ cup finely shredded purple cabbage

Directions:

1. With your parent's help, set the oven temperature to 425°F. Preheat the oven. Place a sheet of aluminum foil or parchment paper on a baking sheet.
2. Lay the pita bread on the baking sheet without overlapping.
3. Spread 1 ½ tablespoons of pizza sauce on each pita bread. Sprinkle half the cheese on each pita.
4. Now place half of each - the tomatoes, sweet potato, broccoli, corn, beetroot, and purple cabbage on one pita in concentric semi-circles like a rainbow.
5. Repeat the same process with the other pita and vegetables.
6. Bake for about 10 – 12 minutes. Slice and serve.

Grilled Cheese Sandwich

Serves: 1

Nutritional values per serving: 1 sandwich

Calories: 400

Fat: 28 g

Carbohydrates: 26 g

Protein: 11 g

Ingredients:
- 2 slices white bread
- 1 slice of cheddar cheese
- 1 ½ tablespoons butter

Directions:
1. Place a non-stick pan over medium heat.

2. Spread half the butter on one side of a bread slice. Place the bread slice in the skillet, with the buttered side down; it should touch the bottom of the pan. Place the cheese slice on the bread.
3. Spread the remaining butter on one side of the other slice of bread and place it on the cheese slice, with the buttered side facing on top.
4. Cook until the underside is light brown or cooked as per your preference.
5. Flip the sides of the sandwich over and cook the other side as well.
6. Place the sandwich on a plate. Cut into the desired shape and serve.

Chicken Salad Sandwiches

Serves: 2

Nutritional values per serving: 1 sandwich

Calories: 430

Fat: 27 g

Carbohydrates: 27 g

Protein: 19 g

Ingredients:

- ¾ cup cooked, chopped chicken or turkey
- ½ small onion, finely chopped
- ⅛ teaspoon pepper
- ¼ cup chopped celery
- ¼ cup mayonnaise
- 4 slices bread

Chapter 6: Pizza, Sandwiches, And Burgers

- ⅛ teaspoon salt

Directions:

1. Combine chicken, onion, pepper, celery, mayonnaise, and salt in a bowl.
2. Place half the chicken mixture on each of 2 bread slices. Cover with the remaining 2 bread slices to complete the sandwich.
3. Cut into the desired shape and serve.

CHAPTER 7
ONE POT MEALS

Chicken Stew

Serves: 2

Nutritional value per serving: ½ recipe

Calories: 362

Fat: 11.4 g

Carbohydrates: 19.8 g

Protein: 44 g

Ingredients:

- 1 tablespoon butter
- ½ stalk celery, chopped
- 2 cloves garlic, peeled, minced
- ¾ pound boneless, skinless chicken breasts
- 2 small bay leaves
- 1 ½ cups low-sodium chicken broth

- 1 large carrot, peeled, cut into thin round slices
- Salt to taste
- ½ tablespoon all-purpose flour
- 2 sprigs thyme
- 6 ounces baby potatoes, scrubbed, quartered
- Chopped fresh parsley to garnish
- Freshly ground black pepper to taste

Directions:

1. Add butter to a pot. Place the pot over medium heat. When butter melts, add celery, carrot, salt, and pepper and stir.
2. Stir often until the vegetables are slightly soft, about 3 minutes. Stir in the garlic. Keep stirring for about 30 seconds until you get a nice aroma.
3. Sprinkle flour all over the vegetables and stir. Stir in thyme sprigs, potatoes, chicken, bay leaves, and broth. Add salt and pepper to taste.
4. Simmer until the chicken and potatoes are cooked. Turn off the heat.
5. Fish out the chicken with a slotted spoon and place it on your cutting board. Shred the chicken with a pair of forks into smaller pieces. Add the shredded chicken to the pot.
6. Sprinkle parsley on top and serve.

Chicken Enchilada Bake

Serves: 5

Nutritional values per serving: 1 cup

Calories: 428

Fat: 27 g

Carbohydrates: 16 g

Protein: 32 g

Ingredients:

- 2 ¼ cups shredded rotisserie chicken
- 10 tablespoons sour cream
- 2 cups shredded Monterey Jack cheese
- ½ can (from a 28-ounce can) of green enchilada sauce
- 4-5 corn tortillas, torn into about 1 ½ inch pieces
- Chopped parsley to garnish (optional)

Chapter 7: One Pot Meals

Directions:

1. With your parent's help, set the oven temperature to 375°F. Preheat the oven.
2. Grease a small, square, or rectangular baking dish (about 6 – 7 inches) with cooking oil spray.
3. Spread half the chicken on the bottom of the baking dish. Spread half the enchilada sauce over the chicken. Drizzle half the sour cream over the enchilada sauce layer.
4. Place half the tortilla pieces over the sour cream layer. Sprinkle half the cheese on top.
5. Now repeat these layers once again (steps 3 and 4).
6. Cover the baking dish with aluminum foil. Place it in the oven and set the timer for about 40 minutes.
7. Remove the foil and continue baking for another 10 minutes.
8. Cool for about 10 minutes. Garnish with parsley and serve.

Greek Turkey and Rice Skillet

Serves: 2

Nutritional value per serving:

1 ¾ cups

Calories: 600.1

Fat: 34.8 g

Carbohydrates: 43 g

Protein: 27.9 g

Ingredients:

- ½ tablespoon olive oil
- 9.5 ounces 97% lean ground turkey
- ⅛ teaspoon salt
- ½ cup long-grain white rice
- 3 tablespoon sun-dried tomato halves

- ¾ cup chicken broth
- ½ lemon
- 1 clove garlic, peeled, minced
- ½ teaspoon dried oregano
- Freshly cracked pepper to taste
- 1 cup spinach leaves, fresh or frozen
- ¼ cup kalamata olives, sliced
- Chopped parsley to garnish
- 1 tablespoon feta cheese

Directions:

1. Pour oil into a skillet and place the skillet over medium heat. When the oil is hot, add garlic and keep stirring for about a minute or until you get a nice aroma. Make sure you do not burn the garlic.
2. Stir in the turkey, pepper, salt, and oregano. As you stir, break the meat into smaller crumbles.
3. When the turkey is cooked, add rice, sun-dried tomatoes, spinach, and olives and mix well.
4. Pour the chicken broth into the skillet and give it a good stir.
5. Cover the skillet and increase the heat to medium-high. When it starts boiling, turn down the heat to low and simmer until the rice is cooked. Stir occasionally.
6. While the rice is cooking, grate half of the lemon rind. Squeeze the juice out of the lemon.
7. Mix well. Add lemon juice and mix well. Garnish with lemon rind, feta, and parsley and serve.

One-pan Fish and Rice

Serves: 2

Nutritional values per serving: ½ recipe

Calories: 484

Fat: 12 g

Carbohydrates: 66.7 g

Protein: 31.2 g

Ingredients:

- 2 white fish filets (4.5 ounces each), skinless, pin-boned
- 6.2 ounces ripe assorted colored cherry tomatoes, halved
- 5.3 ounces long grain white basmati rice
- 3 heaping teaspoons of green olive tapenade
- A handful of fresh basil leaves, torn
- 10 ounces water

- Salt to taste
- ½ tablespoon olive oil
- ½ tablespoon red wine vinegar
- Black pepper to taste
- Extra-virgin olive oil to drizzle

Directions:
1. Place a shallow casserole pan over high heat.
2. Add rice and 1 heaping teaspoon of tapenade and stir until well combined.
3. Mix well with tomatoes, olive oil, and red wine vinegar in another bowl.
4. Add water to the pan. Cover with the lid. Add salt, pepper, and most of the basil leaves when it starts boiling. Stir well.
5. Now place the fish filets in the pan. Now push the filets into the rice.
6. Spread the tomatoes with the marinade over the fish and rice.
7. Cover the pan once again and cook until the rice is tender. Uncover and cook for another minute or two.
8. Spread a heaping teaspoon of tapenade on each fish filet. Scatter the remaining basil leaves on top.
9. Trickle some extra-virgin olive oil on top and serve.

Hamburger Casserole

Serves: 5

Nutritional values per serving: 1 cup

Calories: 270

Fat: 8 g

Carbohydrates: 5 g

Protein: 21 g

Ingredients:

- 1 pound 90% lean ground beef
- ½ large onion, sliced
- ¼ teaspoon pepper
- ½ cup boiling water
- Chopped fresh parsley to garnish (optional)
- 2 pounds potatoes, peeled, cut into ¼ inch thick sliced

Chapter 7: One Pot Meals

- ½ teaspoon salt
- ½ teaspoon beef bouillon granules
- 1 can (14 ounces) diced tomatoes with their liquid

Directions:
1. Take a small, heavy pan or a Dutch oven. Place half the meat on the bottom of the pan.
2. Layer with half the potatoes, followed by half the onions.
3. Season with ¼ teaspoon salt and ⅛ teaspoon pepper.
4. Place the remaining meat over the onions, then the remaining potatoes, and, finally, onions.
5. Combine beef bouillon granules in boiling water. Drizzle this all over the meat and vegetables. Spread the tomatoes on top.
6. Cover the pan and place it over medium heat. Cook until the meat and potatoes are tender.
7. Sprinkle parsley on top if you are using and serving.

CHAPTER 8
SHEET PAN RECIPES

Chicken Nuggets

Serves: 3

Nutritional values per serving: ⅓ recipe

Calories: 308

Fat: 19 g

Carbohydrates: 15 g

Protein: 19 g

Ingredients:
- 3 skinless, boneless chicken breast halves
- 2 tablespoons grated parmesan cheese
- ½ teaspoon dried thyme
- ¼ cup melted butter
- ½ cup Italian seasoned breadcrumbs
- ½ teaspoon dried basil

- ½ teaspoon salt

Directions:
1. Under the guidance of an adult, set the oven temperature to 400° F. Preheat the oven.
2. Spray some cooking oil spray on a baking sheet.
3. Add breadcrumbs, thyme, basil, salt, and parmesan into a bowl. Stir until well combined.
4. To melt the butter, you can do it in a microwave or a small pan over low heat. To melt in a microwave, place butter in a microwave-safe bowl and place it in the microwave. Set the timer for about 30 seconds. If it is not fully melted, cook for another 10 to 15 seconds. To melt in a pan, place butter in a pan and place it over low heat until the butter melts.
5. Place the melted butter in a bowl.
6. Take one piece of chicken and dip it in butter. Now lift the chicken piece. Shake the chicken piece to drip excess butter. Next, dredge the chicken piece in the breadcrumbs and place it on the prepared baking sheet.
7. Repeat the process with the remaining chicken pieces (previous step). Do not overlap the chicken pieces.
8. Place the baking sheet in the oven for about 20 minutes or until brown on the outside and cooked inside.
9. Serve hot with a dip of your choice.

Parmesan Chicken

Serves: 3

Nutritional values per serving:

Calories: 546

Fat: 36 g

Carbohydrates: 1 g

Protein: 51 g

Ingredients:

- 3 chicken breasts
- ⅓ cup grated parmesan cheese
- ¼ teaspoon pepper
- ½ cup light mayonnaise or Greek yogurt
- ¾ teaspoon seasoning salt
- ½ teaspoon garlic powder

Directions:

1. With the help of an adult, set the oven temperature to 400° F. Preheat the oven.
2. Grease a baking sheet with some cooking oil spray.
3. Place chicken on the baking sheet.
4. Mix well with a bowl of mayonnaise, pepper, salt, garlic powder, and half the cheese.
5. Smear the mixture over the chicken pieces. Scatter the remaining parmesan over the chicken.
6. Place it in the oven for baking for about 45 minutes or until the chicken is cooked through. Insert a meat thermometer or an instant-read thermometer in the thickest part of the meat. The cooked chicken should have an internal temperature of 165° F.
7. Serve.

Sheet-Pan Steak & Potatoes

Serves: 2

Nutritional values per serving: ½ recipe

Calories: 415

Fat: 21 g

Carbohydrates: 22 g

Protein: 35 g

Ingredients:

- ½ pound potatoes cut into ½ inch wedges
- Salt to taste
- 2 cups chopped asparagus
- ¼ teaspoon garlic powder
- 1 heaping tablespoon of crumbled blue cheese
- 1 tablespoon extra-virgin olive oil, divided

Chapter 8: Sheet Pan Recipes

- Pepper to taste
- 10 ounces skirt steak, trimmed
- ¼ teaspoon dried rosemary

Directions:

1. Under the guidance of an adult, set the oven temperature to 425° F. Preheat the oven.
2. Spray some cooking oil spray lightly on a baking sheet.
3. Place potatoes in a bowl. Drizzle ½ tablespoon of oil over the potatoes. Sprinkle some salt and pepper and toss well.
4. Transfer the potatoes to the baking sheet and spread the potatoes. Place the baking sheet in the oven for 15 minutes and bake.
5. Place asparagus in the same bowl in which the potatoes were placed. Drizzle ½ tablespoon of oil over the asparagus and toss well. Sprinkle salt and pepper and toss well.
6. Scatter the asparagus on the baking sheet with potatoes.
7. Season the steak with salt, pepper, garlic powder, and rosemary, and keep it over the vegetables.
8. Place the baking sheet back in the oven and bake for 12 – 15 minutes or until the steak and vegetables are cooked.

Pork Chop Sheet Pan Dinner

Serves: 2

Nutritional values per serving: 1 pork chop with half the vegetables

Calories: 493

Fat: 24 g

Carbohydrates: 35 g

Protein: 36 g

Ingredients:

For the pork chops:
- 1 tablespoon olive oil
- 1 teaspoon brown sugar
- ¼ teaspoon salt or add more to suit your taste
- ¼ teaspoon pepper or to taste

Chapter 8: Sheet Pan Recipes

- ½ tablespoon smoked paprika
- ½ teaspoon garlic powder
- 2 medium boneless pork chops

For the vegetables:

- 3 medium potatoes, peeled, cut into 1-inch cubes
- ½ cup frozen green beans
- ½ cup frozen baby carrots
- 1 tablespoon olive oil
- ½ teaspoon garlic powder
- Salt to taste
- Pepper to taste
- 1 teaspoon lemon juice
- 1 teaspoon dried parsley or 1 tablespoon chopped fresh parsley plus extra fresh parsley to garnish

Directions:

1. With the help of an adult, set the oven temperature to 400° F. Preheat the oven.
2. In a small bowl, combine paprika, garlic powder, pepper, oil, brown sugar, and salt. You will get a paste.
3. Take this paste and rub it all over the pork chops.
4. Place potatoes, green beans, and baby carrots on a baking sheet.
5. Drizzle olive oil and lemon juice over the vegetables. Season with salt, garlic powder, pepper, and parsley, and mix well. Now spread the vegetables in a single layer.
6. Place the pork chops on top of the vegetables. Place it in the oven for about 20 minutes or until the pork is cooked.
7. To check if the pork is cooked through, insert a meat thermometer or an instant-read thermometer in the thickest part of a pork chop. The pork chop is cooked when its internal temperature shows 145° F.
8. Garnish with fresh parsley leaves if desired and serve.

Everything Salmon Sheet Pan Dinner

Serves: 2

Nutritional values per serving: 1 salmon filet with half the vegetables

Calories: 398

Fat: 9 g

Carbohydrates: 42 g

Protein: 31 g

Ingredients:

- 1 medium sweet potato, scrubbed, cut into ¼-inch thick wedges
- ¼ teaspoon salt, divided
- 2 tablespoons Dijon mustard
- ⅛ teaspoon cayenne pepper

- 2 salmon filets (5 ounces each)
- 1 teaspoon soy sauce
- 1 ½ teaspoons olive oil
- ⅛ teaspoon pepper, divided
- 1 tablespoon honey
- 2 ½ cups broccoli florets
- 1 tablespoon of everything bagel seasoning

Directions:
1. Under the guidance of an adult, set the oven temperature to 425° F. Preheat the oven.
2. Place a sheet of foil on a baking sheet. Spray some oil over the foil.
3. Place sweet potatoes in a bowl. Drizzle 1 teaspoon of oil over the sweet potatoes. Sprinkle ⅛ teaspoon salt and half the pepper and toss well.
4. Spread the sweet potatoes on one side of the baking sheet. Place it in the oven and bake for 5 minutes.
5. Place broccoli in the same bowl in which the sweet potatoes were placed.
6. Drizzle ½ teaspoon of oil over the broccoli. Sprinkle the remaining salt and pepper over the broccoli and toss well.
7. Take the baking sheet and spread the broccoli to the sweet potatoes.
8. Combine honey, Dijon mustard, and cayenne pepper in a bowl.
9. Place salmon next to the broccoli. Spread 2 teaspoons of the mustard mixture on each salmon filet. Scatter everything bagel seasoning over the filets and place the baking sheet back in the oven.
10. Bake for about 12 minutes or until the vegetables and salmon are cooked. To check if the salmon is cooked, take a fork

and pierce it into the salmon. If it flakes easily, the salmon is cooked or baked for a few more minutes.
11. To the remaining mustard mixture, add soy sauce and stir. Pour the mustard mixture over the vegetables and mix well.
12. Serve vegetables with salmon filets.

CHAPTER 9
SKILLET RECIPES

Skillet Lasagna

Serves: 3

Nutritional value per serving: ⅓ recipe

Calories: 559

Fat: 31 g

Carbohydrates: 35 g

Protein: 36 g

Ingredients:

- 1 ½ tablespoons olive oil
- 2 cloves garlic, peeled, finely minced
- ¾ tablespoon Italian seasoning
- 4 lasagna noodles, broken
- ½ can (from 15 ounces can) of tomato sauce or marinara sauce

- Salt to taste
- ¼ teaspoon ground black pepper or, to taste
- 1 can (14.5 ounces can) of diced tomatoes with their juice
- ⅓ – ½ cup water
- ¼ heaping cup of ricotta cheese
- A handful of fresh basil leaves chopped
- 1 cup diced onion
- ½ pound ground beef
- 1 cup fresh mozzarella cheese, thinly sliced

Directions:

1. Pour oil into a skillet and place the skillet over medium-high heat.
2. When the oil is hot, add the onion and cook until the onion is slightly soft. Stir on and off.
3. Stir in the garlic. Keep on stirring for about a minute. Stir in the beef. As you stir, break the meat into smaller pieces. Cook until the meat is brown, stirring regularly.
4. Stir in the pepper and Italian seasoning. Scatter lasagna noodles all over the meat mixture. Pour the tomatoes and tomato sauce over the lasagna noodles.
5. Drizzle water all over the ingredients. Keep the pan covered with a lid.
6. Turn down the heat to medium-low and cook until the lasagna noodles are al dente.
7. Give the lasagna a good stir. Scatter ricotta all over the lasagna and stir lightly. Do not over-mix.
8. Bring down the heat to low. Sprinkle mozzarella on top. Cook covered for a couple of minutes.
9. Sprinkle basil on top and serve.

Chicken and Tortellini Pesto Skillet

Serves: 3

Nutritional value per serving:

⅓ recipe

Calories: 634

Fat: 35 g

Carbohydrates: 38 g

Protein: 44 g

Ingredients:

- 1 tablespoon olive oil
- Salt to taste
- Freshly ground pepper to taste
- ¼ cup store-bought pesto
- ½ cup parmesan cheese, divided

Chapter 9: Skillet Recipes

- ¼ cup halved cherry tomatoes
- ¾ pound chicken breast, cut into cubes
- ¼ cup chicken broth
- ¼ cup heavy cream
- ½ cup baby spinach
- ½ package (from a 16 ounces package) refrigerated cheese tortellini

Directions:

1. Pour oil into a skillet and place the skillet over medium-high heat. When the oil is hot, place the chicken in the skillet. Sprinkle salt and pepper over the chicken and stir.
2. Cook until brown all over on the outside and cooked inside.
3. Remove chicken with a slotted spoon and place in a bowl. Cover and keep it aside for now.
4. Turn down the heat to medium. Pour broth into the skillet. Scrape the bottom of the skillet to remove any brown bits that may be stuck.
5. Add heavy cream and pesto and stir.
6. Let it simmer until the sauce is thick.
7. Stir in ¼ cup of cheese. Once the cheese melts, stir in the tomatoes and spinach.
8. Let it cook for about 3 minutes or until the spinach turns limp.
9. Stir in the chicken and tortellini. Heat thoroughly.
10. Transfer into a serving dish. Garnish with remaining cheese and serve.

Spanish Rice

Serves: 2

Nutritional values per serving: 1 ½ cups

Calories: 408

Fat: 12 g

Carbohydrates: 49 g

Protein: 28 g

Ingredients:

- ½ pound 90% lean ground beef
- ½ medium green bell pepper, chopped
- ½ can (from a 14.5 ounces can) unsalted, diced tomatoes, drained
- ½ teaspoon chili powder
- ⅛ teaspoon salt or to taste

Chapter 9: Skillet Recipes

- Thinly sliced green onion to garnish (optional)
- ¼ teaspoon garlic powder
- 1 ⅓ cups cooked brown rice
- ½ large onion, chopped
- ½ can (from a 15 ounces can) tomato sauce
- ½ teaspoon ground cumin

Directions:

1. Place a skillet over medium heat. Add beef, bell pepper, and onion and stir often until the meat is brown. As you stir, break the meat into smaller pieces.
2. Add tomatoes, tomato sauce, cumin, garlic powder, salt, and chili powder and mix well.
3. When the mixture starts boiling, stir in the rice. When the rice is heated thoroughly, turn off the heat.
4. Sprinkle green onions on top and serve.

Skillet Pork Chops With Gravy

Serves: 2

Nutritional values per serving: 1 pork chop with half the gravy, without rice

Calories: 615

Fat: 32 g

Carbohydrates: 39 g

Protein: 47 g

Ingredients:

For the pork chops:

- 2 boneless pork chops (4 ounces each), about 1 – 1 ½ inches thick
- ¼ teaspoon pepper
- ½ tablespoon extra-virgin olive oil

Chapter 9: Skillet Recipes

- ½ teaspoon salt
- 1 teaspoon chopped fresh thyme

For the gravy:

- 1 ½ tablespoons flour
- ½ teaspoon chopped fresh thyme or ⅛ teaspoon dried thyme
- ⅛ teaspoon salt
- 1 ½ tablespoons unsalted butter
- 10 tablespoons low-sodium chicken broth
- ¼ teaspoon pepper
- ½ tablespoon non-fat Greek yogurt or sour cream

Directions:

1. To make pork chops: Place a skillet over medium-high heat. Pour oil into the skillet. Wait for the oil to get hot.
2. Sprinkle thyme, salt, and pepper all over the pork chops and place in the skillet.
3. Cook until the underside of the pork chops is brown, about 3 to 4 minutes.
4. Flip sides and cook the other side until brown, about 3 to 4 minutes.
5. Take out the pork chops from the skillet with a slotted spoon and place on a plate. Keep the pork chops covered.
6. Turn down the heat to medium-low. Now place the butter in the skillet.
7. Stir in the flour. Keep whisking until well combined. This mixture is called roux. Make sure the flour doesn't get burnt or brown. It should be toasted lightly.
8. Whisking constantly, pour the broth into the skillet. Keep whisking until smooth and free from lumps.
9. Add thyme, pepper, and salt. Stir constantly until the gravy is thick.
10. Place the pork chops in the skillet. Spoon some gravy on top of the pork chops as well.

11. Keep the skillet covered with a lid and let it simmer. Now insert a meat thermometer or an instant-read thermometer in the thickest part of the meat. When the meat temperature is 135° F to 140° F on the meat thermometer, you can turn off the heat.
12. Stir in the Greek yogurt.
13. Serve pork chops with gravy. You can serve it over rice.

Chapter 9: Skillet Recipes

Crispy Breaded Tilapia

Serves: 2

Nutritional values per serving: 2 tilapia filet halves

Calories: 246

Fat: 10 g

Carbohydrates: 15 g

Protein: 27 g

Ingredients:
- 6 tablespoons panko breadcrumbs
- ½ teaspoon salt
- ½ tablespoon milk
- 1 tablespoon canola or olive oil
- ⅛ cup chopped fresh parsley
- 1 small egg

- 2 tilapia filets (4 ounces each), cut into 2 halves

Directions:

1. Place panko breadcrumbs, salt, and parsley on a plate and stir until well combined.
2. Crack the egg into a bowl. Add milk and beat until well combined.
3. Take 1 piece of tilapia filet and dip it in the egg mixture. Pick it up and shake it slightly to drip off the excess egg. Place it on a plate. Repeat this process with all the tilapia filet halves.
4. Place a non-stick pan over medium heat. Pour oil into the pan. Wait for the oil to become hot. Place the filets in the pan. Cook until the underside is golden brown.
5. Flip sides and cook until the underside is golden brown and cooked through inside. To check it is cooked inside, take a fork and pierce a piece of tilapia. It should break into flakes easily.
6. Take out the tilapia from the pan and serve right away.

CHAPTER 10
MICROWAVE RECIPES

NOTE: Please learn to operate the microwave with the help of your parents or an adult.

Chocolate Mug Cake

Serves: 2

Nutritional value per serving: 1 slice

Calories: 603

Fat: 30 g

Carbohydrates: 82 g

Protein: 7 g

Ingredients:

- ½ cup all-purpose flour
- 4 tablespoons unsweetened cocoa powder
- ¼ teaspoon salt
- ½ cup white sugar
- ¼ teaspoon baking soda
- 6 tablespoons milk

Chapter 10: Microwave Recipes

- 2 tablespoons water
- 4 tablespoons canola oil
- ½ teaspoon vanilla extract:

Directions:

1. Combine flour, baking soda, cocoa powder, and salt in a large microwave-safe mug. If you do not have a large mug, you can use a small microwave-safe dish.
2. Add milk, water, canola oil, and vanilla extract and stir until smooth.
3. Place the mug in the microwave and cook on High for 2 minutes or until cooked in the center.
4. Cool for a while in the mug itself. Remove the cake from the mug, cut it into 2 halves and serve.

Breakfast Potatoes

Serves: 1

Nutritional value per serving: Entire recipe

Calories: 180

Fat: 4 g

Carbohydrates: 31 g

Protein: 6 g

Ingredients:

- 1 medium potato, peeled, sliced
- ⅛ teaspoon salt
- ⅛ teaspoon garlic salt
- ⅛ cup sliced onion
- Pepper to taste
- ⅛ cup shredded cheddar cheese

Directions:

1. Grease a microwave-safe plate with some cooking oil spray. Place the potato and onion slices on the plate. Sprinkle salt, pepper, and garlic salt over the potato and onion.
2. Cover the plate and place it in the microwave. Cook on High for 8 – 10 minutes or until the potatoes are fork-tender. Sprinkle cheese during the last 30 seconds of cooking.
3. Mix well and serve.

Meat Loaf

Serves: 4

Nutritional value per serving:

1 slice

Calories: 382

Fat: 19 g

Carbohydrates: 23 g

Protein: 30 g

Ingredients:

- ½ cup tomato sauce
- ½ teaspoon prepared mustard
- ¼ cup saltine cracker crumbs
- 1 large egg, lightly beaten
- ⅛ teaspoon ground black pepper or more to taste

Chapter 10: Microwave Recipes

- 1 pound extra-lean ground beef
- ⅛ cup brown sugar
- ½ medium onion, minced
- ⅛ cup minced green bell pepper
- ½ teaspoon salt
- ⅛ teaspoon garlic powder

Directions:

1. Add brown sugar, tomato sauce, and mustard into a bowl and stir until the sugar dissolves.
2. Add onion, bell pepper, salt, garlic powder, cracker crumbs, egg, and pepper into a mixing bowl and stir until well incorporated.
3. Stir in beef and half the tomato sauce mixture. Once the mixture is well combined, spread the mixture into a microwave-safe dish.
4. Spoon the remaining tomato sauce mixture over the meat. Spread it evenly.
5. Place the dish in the microwave and cook on high for about 8– 15 minutes or until the internal temperature of the meatloaf in the center shows 165° F on the meat thermometer.
6. The meatloaf should not be pink anymore, and the juices will be released when the meatloaf is cooked. This is another sign to check if the meatloaf is cooked.
7. Take out the dish from the microwave and discard any cooked fat from the dish. Let it rest for about 12 – 15 minutes. Do not cover the dish while it is resting.
8. Cut into 4 equal slices and serve.

Deli Roast Beef Sandwiches with Mashed Potatoes

Serves: 2

Nutritional value per serving:

1 open-faced sandwich with ¾ cup meat mixture and ½ cup mashed potatoes

Calories: 347

Fat: 7 g

Carbohydrates: 38 g

Protein: 30 g

Ingredients:

- ½ pound deli roast beef sliced
- ½ can (from a 4-ounce can) of mushrooms, sliced, drained
- 2 slices (½ inch thick) Italian bread

Chapter 10: Microwave Recipes

- 1 can (10. 25 ounces each) beef gravy
- ½ package (from a 3 ¾ ounces package) of creamy butter instant mashed potatoes

Directions:

1. Place beef, mushrooms, and beef gravy in a microwave-safe bowl and place it in the microwave. Cover the bowl and cook on high for 2 minutes.
2. In the meantime, follow the directions given on the package and cook the mashed potatoes.
3. Divide the meat mixture equally and spread over the bread slices. Divide the mashed potatoes equally and place them alongside each plate.

Beef and Cheese Enchiladas

Serves: 1

Nutritional value per serving: Entire recipe, without serving options

Calories: 538

Fat: 32 g

Carbohydrates: 34 g

Protein: 34 g

Ingredients:

- ½ cup ground beef crumbled
- ⅔ cup shredded cheddar cheese, divided
- 1 teaspoon canned chopped green chilies
- ⅔ tablespoon chopped onion
- ⅓ cup enchilada sauce, divided

Chapter 10: Microwave Recipes

- 2 corn tortillas (6 ounces each) warmed

To serve: Optional
- Shredded lettuce
- Sour cream

Directions:
1. Place onion and beef in a microwave-safe dish and place it in the microwave.
2. Cover the dish and cook for about 2 to 3 minutes or until the meat is not pink anymore.
3. Drain off any cooked fat that is in the dish. Add ⅓ cup of cheese, 1 – 2 tablespoons of enchilada sauce, and the green chilies and mix well.
4. Divide the meat mixture equally among the tortillas. You should get around ½ cup of the meat mixture for each tortilla. Place it along the diameter of the tortillas.
5. Grease a microwave-safe dish with some cooking spray.
6. Roll the tortillas and place them in the greased dish with the seam side down. Spread the remaining enchilada sauce over the enchiladas. Cover the dish.
7. Place the dish in the microwave and cook on high for about 3 minutes or until it is well heated.
8. Sprinkle the remaining cheese on top, and do not cover the dish.
9. Cook for about a minute or until the cheese melts.
10. Drizzle sour cream on top and serve enchiladas with lettuce if desired.

CHAPTER 11
SNACK RECIPES

Mustard Pretzel Nuggets

Serves: 8

Nutritional value per serving: ¾ cup

Calories: 204

Fat: 0 g

Carbohydrates: 43 g

Protein: 5 g

Ingredients:

- 12 cups sourdough pretzel nuggets
- 4 tablespoons honey
- 1 teaspoon onion powder
- 1 teaspoon ground mustard
- ⅔ cup prepared mustard
- 2 tablespoons cider vinegar

- 1 teaspoon garlic powder

Directions:
1. This is one of the storable snacks that are very tasty. Preheat the oven to 350° F with the help of an adult. Coat a baking dish with some cooking spray.
2. Combine honey, onion powder, ground mustard, prepared mustard, cider vinegar, and garlic powder in a bowl.
3. Add pretzels and stir until the pretzels are well coated with the honey mustard mixture.
4. Place the pretzels in the baking dish and spread them evenly. Place it in the oven and set the timer for 15 to 20 minutes or until the pretzels are light brown and crispy.
5. Make sure to stir the pretzels every 5 minutes.
6. Let the pretzels cool in the baking dish on a wire rack.
7. Transfer the pretzels into an airtight container. It can last for 4 – 5 days.

Peanut Butter-Oat Energy Balls

Serves: 6

Nutritional value per serving: 1 energy ball

Calories: 73

Fat: 3 g

Carbohydrates: 10 g

Protein: 2 g

Ingredients:

- 6 medjool dates, pitted, chopped
- 2 tablespoons natural peanut butter
- ¼ cup rolled oats
- Chia seeds to garnish (optional)

Chapter 11: Snack Recipes

Directions:
1. Take some hot water in a bowl. Drop the pitted dates into the bowl. Let them soak for about 10 minutes. Drain off the water.
2. Add dates, peanut butter, and oats into a blender and give short pulses until chopped into fine pieces.
3. Make 6 equal portions of the mixture. Shape each portion into a ball. Sprinkle chia seeds on top and place on a plate. Place it in the refrigerator until ready to serve.

Antipasto Skewers

Serves: 6

Nutritional value per serving:

1 skewer, without vinaigrette

Calories: 204

Fat: 9 g

Carbohydrates: 24 g

Protein: 11 g

Ingredients:

- 12 grape tomatoes
- 6 thin slices of hard salami
- Italian vinaigrette (optional)
- 1 cup cherry size fresh mozzarella cheese balls
- 6 pimento-stuffed Queen olives

Chapter 11: Snack Recipes

Directions:
1. Take 6 wooden skewers (6 inches each). Divide the tomatoes, salami, cheese balls, and olives equally and thread them onto the skewers in any colorful manner you please. Fold the salami while threading them.
2. Place the built skewers on a plate. Drizzle vinaigrette over the skewers if using and serve.
3. You can use any other vinaigrette of your choice if desired.

Sausage Cheese Puffs

Serves: 24

Nutritional value per serving: 1 puff without serving options

Calories: 89

Fat: 6 g

Carbohydrates: 6 g

Protein: 4 g

Ingredients:
- ½ pound bulk Italian sausage
- 2 cups shredded cheddar cheese
- 1 ½ cups biscuit/baking mix
- ⅛ cup + ¼ cup water

To serve:
- Jam

Chapter 11: Snack Recipes

- Jelly
- Honey
- Flavored maple syrup

Directions:
1. Preheat the oven to 400° F with the help of an adult.
2. Add sausage to a skillet and place it over medium heat. As it cooks, stir the meat and break it into smaller pieces. When the meat is not pink, turn off the heat and discard any cooked fat from the skillet.
3. Add biscuit mix and cheese into a bowl and stir until well combined.
4. Add water and sausage and stir using the help of a fork until well combined.
5. Make 24 equal portions of the mixture and shape each portion into a ball. Place the sausage balls on a baking sheet. Do not grease the baking sheet.
6. Place the baking sheet in the oven and set the timer for about 12 minutes or until golden brown. They will puff up on baking.
7. Place the sausage balls on a wire rack to cool.
8. You can freeze the baked puffs in freezer-safe bags. Heat them in a preheated oven for 7 to 8 minutes and serve. There is no need to defrost them.
9. You can serve with any of the suggested serving options.

Chicken and Bacon Roll-Ups

Serves: 24

Nutritional value per serving: 1 roll-up

Calories: 43

Fat: 2 g

Carbohydrates: 4 g

Protein: 3 g

Ingredients:

- ½ can (from 9.75 ounces can) a chunk of white chicken, drained
- ½ cup salsa, divided
- 3 flour tortillas (8 inches each) at room temperature
- 4 ounces garden vegetable cream cheese spread
- 2 precooked bacon strips, crumbled

Chapter 11: Snack Recipes

Directions:
1. Add cream cheese spread, chicken, bacon, and half the salsa into a bowl and stir well.
2. Divide the mixture equally among the tortillas and spread it evenly.
3. Roll the tortillas tightly and keep them wrapped with cling wrap. Chill until ready to serve.
4. This is to be served chilled.
5. Remove the cling wrap and cut each wrap into 8 equal slices.
6. Place them on a serving platter. Place remaining salsa alongside and serve.

CHAPTER 12
SIDES RECIPES

Oven Baked Sweet Potato Fries

Serves: 3

Nutritional values per serving: ⅓ recipe

Calories: 203

Fat: 7 g

Carbohydrates: 33 g

Protein: 3 g

Ingredients:
- 1 pound gold sweet potatoes (orange flesh)
- ¾ teaspoon salt
- 1 ½ tablespoons extra-virgin olive oil
- ½ to 1 tablespoon spice blend of your choice, like Cajun seasoning, peri, etc.

Chapter 12: Sides Recipes

Directions:
1. Place a roasting pan in the oven. Preheat the oven to 450° F with the help of an adult. The roasting pan should also be preheated.
2. Using a peeler, peel the sweet potatoes. Slice off the ends. Cut each sweet potato into 2 halves lengthwise.
3. Cut into about ¼ to ½ inch thick wedges. Place them in a bowl. Drizzle oil over the sweet potatoes. Add salt and the chosen spice blend and mix until well combined using your hand.
4. Remove the roasting pan from the oven and place the sweet potato wedges in the roasting pan without overlapping.
5. Place it in the oven and set the timer for about 20 minutes or until golden brown. Turn the sweet potatoes over after baking for about 10 minutes.
6. Remove the fries from the oven and let them rest for 5 minutes.
7. Serve.

Crispy Baked Onion Rings

Serves: 3

Nutritional values per serving: ⅓ recipe

Calories: 267

Fat: 5.8 g

Carbohydrates: 44.6 g

Protein: 10 g

Ingredients:
- 1 large egg
- ½ cup flour
- 1 medium sweet onion, peeled, cut into ½-inch thick, round slices
- ½ tablespoon mayonnaise
- ½ teaspoon cayenne pepper

Chapter 12: Sides Recipes

- Salt to taste
- Pepper to taste
- 1 cup Italian-style breadcrumbs

Directions:
1. Preheat the oven to 450° F with the help of an adult.
2. Grease a baking sheet with a generous amount of cooking spray.
3. Add flour, salt, cayenne pepper, and pepper into a bowl and stir well.
4. Crack the egg into a bowl. Add mayonnaise and whisk until smooth.
5. Place panko breadcrumbs in a shallow bowl.
6. Push your finger through the onion rounds and separate the rings.
7. Take one onion ring and coat it in the flour mixture. Now dip it in the egg. Pick it up and shake the ring slightly to drip off the excess egg. Next, dredge the onion rings in the breadcrumbs. Place it on the baking sheet.
8. Repeat this process with all the onion rings (the previous step).
9. Spray a generous amount of cooking spray over the onion rings. Place the baking sheet in the oven and bake until they turn golden brown. Flip sides after baking for about 7 to 8 minutes.
10. Serve hot.

Baked French Fries

Serves: 2

Nutritional values per serving: ½ recipe

Calories: 357

Fat: 14 g

Carbohydrates: 55 g

Protein: 5 g

Ingredients:

- 2 large baking potatoes
- 1 teaspoon paprika (optional)
- 1 teaspoon chili powder (optional)
- 1 teaspoon garlic powder
- 1 teaspoon onion powder
- ½ teaspoon salt or seasoned salt or lemon pepper

Chapter 12: Sides Recipes

- 2 tablespoons olive oil

Directions:

1. Under the supervision of an adult, set the oven temperature to 450° F.
2. You will learn to cut the potato into fries: Cut a thin slice from one of the edges of a potato. Place the potato on your cutting board so the cut part is on the cutting board. Cut thin slices lengthwise (depending on the thickness of the fries).
3. Place 2 to 3 slices together in a stack and cut into thin sticks lengthwise if you want long fries or widthwise if you want short fries.
4. Repeat the process with the other potato (steps 2 and 3).
5. Place the potatoes in a bowl. Drizzle oil over the potatoes. Sprinkle chili powder, paprika, garlic powder, onion powder, seasoned salt, and mix well. Transfer the potatoes to the baking sheet, spreading them out.
6. Place the baking sheet in the oven and set the timer for 20 minutes. Stir the fries after 10 minutes.
7. Continue baking until they are crisp and golden brown.
8. Serve hot.

Ants On A Log

Serves: 3

Nutritional values per serving: ⅓ recipe

Calories: 71

Fat: 5 g

Carbohydrates: 4 g

Protein: 2 g

Ingredients:

- 1 ½ celery sticks
- 15 raisins
- 2 tablespoons peanut butter

Directions:

1. Cut the whole celery stick into 2 halves. So, including the ½ celery stick, you have 3 celery pieces which are your logs.
2. Fill peanut butter in the hollow part of the celery sticks.
3. Place 5 raisins on each log and press it into the peanut butter. The raisins are the ants.
4. You can serve it at room temperature or chilled.

Quick Broccoli and Cheese

Serves: 2

Nutritional values per serving:

Calories: 182

Fat: 11 g

Carbohydrates: 11 g

Protein: 12 g

Ingredients:
- ½ cup water
- 2 cups broccoli florets

For the cheese sauce:
- ½ cup milk
- ½ cup shredded cheddar cheese
- Salt to taste

- Pepper to taste
- ½ tablespoon cornstarch
- ½ tablespoon grated parmesan cheese

Directions:
1. Place the broccoli in a non-stick pan. Pour water into the pan.
2. Place the pan over medium heat. When it starts simmering, cover the pan with a lid. Let it cook for about 3 minutes or until they turn bright green.
3. Transfer the broccoli to a bowl. Drain off the cooked water, if any.
4. To make the cheese sauce: Add cornstarch and milk into a bowl and whisk until smooth.
5. Add the milk mixture to the pan. Keep whisking until the sauce is thick.
6. Bring down the heat to low. Stir in the cheese. Keep whisking until the cheese melts and the sauce is smooth.
7. Add salt and pepper to taste. Pour the cheese sauce over the broccoli. Stir and serve.

CHAPTER 13
DESSERT RECIPES

Fairy Cakes

Serves: 12

Nutritional value per serving: 1 fairy cake

Calories: 144

Fat: 9 g

Carbohydrates: 15 g

Protein: 2 g

Ingredients:

- ½ cup softened butter
- ¾ cup + ⅛ cup self-rising flour
- ½ cup white sugar
- 2 large eggs, beaten

Directions:

1. Under the guidance of an adult, preheat the oven to 350° F.
2. Coat a muffin pan of 12 counts with some cooking oil spray. Place disposable liners in the muffin cups.
3. Place butter and sugar in a bowl. Beat with an electric hand mixer until creamy and smooth.
4. Beat in half the flour and an egg. Once it is smooth, add the remaining egg and flour and beat until smooth.
5. Divide the batter among the muffin cups. Fill it up to ¾ and not more.
6. Place the muffin pan in the oven and set the timer for 10 – 12 minutes or until they are baked. Once they are well baked, they should spring back lightly when you press the top.
7. Let the cakes cool in the muffin pan for 5 minutes. Remove the cakes from the pan and place on a wire rack to cool completely.
8. Serve. You can store extra cakes in an airtight container at room temperature for about 3 – 4 days or in the refrigerator for about 7 – 8 days.

Strawberry Ice Cream

Serves: 4

Nutritional value per serving: ¼ recipe

Calories: 126

Fat: 8. 5 g

Carbohydrates: 12.2 g

Protein: 0.9 g

Ingredients:

- ¾ cup heavy cream
- 3 tablespoons powdered sugar
- 2 cups frozen strawberries or any other frozen berries of your choice
- ½ teaspoon vanilla extract

Directions:

1. Place heavy cream, powdered sugar, strawberries, and vanilla extract in a blender and blend until smooth and of soft serve consistency.
2. Divide into 4 bowls and serve right away.
3. If you do not want to serve immediately, transfer it into a freezer-safe container and freeze it until use.

Pudding Dirt Cups

Serves: 5

Nutritional values per serving: 1 cup

Calories: 285

Fat: 11 g

Carbohydrates: 45 g

Protein: 3 g

Ingredients:
- 1 cup cold milk
- 4 ounces frozen whipped topping, thawed
- 10 gummy worms
- ½ package (from 3.9 ounces 4 servings package) instant chocolate pudding
- ¾ cup crushed chocolate sandwich cookies, divided

Chapter 13: Dessert Recipes

Directions:
1. Place instant chocolate pudding mix in a bowl. Add milk and whisk until the pudding mixture dissolves. Set it aside for about 5 minutes. During this time, it will become thicker.
2. Now add frozen whipped topping and ¼ cup of the cookies.
3. Distribute the pudding into five cups. Scatter the remaining crushed cookies on top of the pudding. Place 2 gummy worms on top of each cup.
4. Place the cups in the refrigerator for about 2 hours or until you need to serve.

Brownies

Serves: 15

Nutritional values per serving: 1 brownie

Calories: 231

Fat: 8.7 g

Carbohydrates: 37.8 g

Protein: 2.2 g

Ingredients:

For the brownies:

- ½ cup melted butter
- 2 teaspoons vanilla extract
- 2 eggs
- 1 cup granulated sugar
- ¼ cup cocoa powder

Chapter 13: Dessert Recipes

- 1 cup all-purpose flour

For the frosting:
- ⅛ cup butter at room temperature
- ⅛ cup milk
- ⅛ cup cocoa powder
- 1 ¼ cups powdered sugar

Directions:
1. Under the guidance of an adult, preheat the oven to 350° F.
2. Place a sheet of foil on a square or rectangular baking sheet. Spray some cooking oil spray over the foil.
3. To melt the butter, you can do it in a microwave or a small pan over low heat. To melt in a microwave, place butter in a microwave-safe bowl and place it in the microwave. Set the timer for about 30 seconds. If it is not fully melted, cook for another 10 to 15 seconds. To melt in a pan, place butter in a pan and place it over low heat until the butter melts.
4. Place the melted butter in a mixing bowl. Add cocoa powder. Using an electric hand mixer, under the guidance of an adult, mix until smooth using medium speed.
5. Crack the eggs into the bowl of butter and add vanilla. Beat for about a minute.
6. Beat in the sugar. Beat until well combined and smooth.
7. Add flour and beat until just incorporated.
8. Spoon the batter into the baking dish and place it in the oven for about 20 to 25 minutes or until set in the middle.
9. Take out the baking dish and let it cool for about 15 to 20 minutes.
10. Meanwhile, make the frosting: Add butter and cocoa powder into a bowl and beat until smooth.
11. Beat in the milk and powdered sugar until smooth. Spoon the frosting over the brownies.

12. Cut into 15 equal portions and serve. Leftover brownies can be stored in an airtight container at room temperature for about 3 days or in the refrigerator for about a week.

Chapter 13: Dessert Recipes

Cookie Ice Cream Sandwiches

Serves: 6

Nutritional values per serving: 1 ice cream sandwich

Calories: 515

Fat: 29 g

Carbohydrates: 61 g

Protein: 7 g

Ingredients:

- ½ package (from a 15.25 ounces package) of chocolate cake mix
- 1 egg
- ¼ cup butterscotch chips
- 1 quart vanilla ice cream, softened
- ¼ cup butter at room temperature

- ¼ cup semi-sweet chocolate chips
- ½ teaspoon vanilla extract

Directions:

1. With the help of an adult, preheat the oven to 350° F. Spray lightly some cooking spray on a baking sheet.
2. Add cake mix, egg, butterscotch chips, butter, chocolate chips, and vanilla into a bowl and mix until dough is formed. Make 12 equal portions of the dough.
3. Place the dough balls on the baking sheet, leaving a sufficient gap between them. Flatten them a bit.
4. Place the baking sheet in the oven and set the timer for 10 minutes, making sure not to bake for longer than this. You want soft but set cookies.
5. After the timer goes off, take out the baking sheet and allow the cookies to cool on the baking sheet for about 6 to 7 minutes.
6. Slide a metal spatula beneath the cookies to loosen them. Now place the cookies directly on a wire rack to cool completely.
7. Place a scoop of ice cream between 2 cookies on the baking sheet. Do this process with all the cookies and ice cream. You must be quick while doing so, or the ice cream will melt away.
8. Place the baking sheet in the freezer until the ice cream is hardened.
9. They can last for about 2 weeks.
10. Serve.

CONCLUSION

Thank you once again for choosing this book. I hope you enjoyed the different recipes given in this book.

Learning to cook is one of the most basic skills that everyone should know. Regardless of your age, there is no such thing as starting too young when it comes to cooking. When you learn to cook, it teaches you more about healthy eating. You can become conscious about the foods you eat. It allows you to fend for yourself and boosts your self-confidence. It will also make you feel more independent. So, there's plenty to gain by learning to cook. Cooking is not something you can master overnight but with a little practice and patience, you will soon start feeling like a pro in the kitchen.

Whether for yourself, your family, or even friends, serving them delicious and home-cooked meals is a perfectly achievable goal. All the information needed to achieve this goal was discussed in this book. From smoothies and breakfast recipes to soups, pizza, sandwiches, snacks, and desserts, there is plenty to explore. You can easily cook your favorite meals within no time once you are equipped with the recipes given in this book. All the recipes given in this book are perfect for beginners to get started. You don't need any fancy ingredients to cook, and you certainly don't have to spend hours together in the kitchen. Take some time and go through the different recipes given in this book. Make a note of the ones you want to try or are excited to cook. Don't forget to stock your pantry with the required ingredients!

You need to follow three simple steps to whip up food like a pro. The first step is to pick a recipe and carefully go through all the instructions given in it. The second step is to gather the needed ingredients and any other tools to cook it. The third step is to simply follow the instructions given in the recipe. Once you follow these three steps, cooking becomes a breeze. Once you get the hang of different flavor combinations and basic techniques, don't hesitate to experiment in the kitchen. Your favorite dishes are only. A few moments away!

The next time you have your friends over, why don't you surprise them with something you cooked? Or maybe you can cook for your family and loved ones! The options are truly endless once you figure out your way around the kitchen. One of the most important things you must remember while cooking is to have fun! Stay safe and have fun in the kitchen!

So, what are you waiting for? It's time to get started!

Thank you and all the best!

REFERENCES

Barclay, L. (n.d.). *Recipes for teenagers*. BBC Good Food. https://www.bbcgoodfood.com/howto/guide/recipes-teenagers

Buiano, M. (2022, May 18). *13 Super Easy Meals Teens Can Make Themselves*. Martha Stewart. https://www.marthastewart.com/1505773/13-super-easy-meals-teens-can-make-themselves

Hansen, C. (2022, January 5). *34 Recipes Teens Should Know By Heart*. Taste of Home. https://www.tasteofhome.com/collection/recipes-kids-should-know-heart/

Katrina. (2022, April 11). *27 Easy dinners that teenagers can cook*. The Organised Housewife. https://theorganisedhousewife.com.au/meal-planning/19-easy-recipes-that-teenagers-can-cook/

Totosegis, D. (2021, October 26). *26 Easy And Healthy Recipes For Teenagers To Cook*. MomJunction. https://www.momjunction.com/articles/easy-recipes-cooking-for-teenagers_00782578/

Printed in Great Britain
by Amazon